CW00519591

Two Vagabond Poet Two Vaga

Series editor: Colin Waters

fault line

Gerry Loose

Vagabond Voices
Glasgow

Published on 22 September 2014 by
Vagabond Voices Publishing Ltd.,
Glasgow,

Scotland.

ISBN: 978-1-908251-34-3

Printed and bound in Poland

Cover design by Mark Mechan

Typeset by Park Productions

The publisher acknowledges subsidy towards
this publication from Creative Scotland

For further information on Vagabond Voices, see the website,

www.vagabondvoices.co.uk

An oar is also a winnowing shovel

Acknowledgements

These poems first appeared in the newspapers, journals & anthologies International Literary Quarterly, Dark Mountain, halfcircle, Tuli ja Savu, Free Verse, Gists and Piths, Foma & Fontanelles, Catapult to Mars, Infinite Editions, painted, spoken, Northwords Now, Truck, Southlight, Entanglements, The Scotsman, Vilenica Almanac and 作家. Some were broadcast on BBC Radio Scotland: my thanks to the editors and broadcasters.

The writing of this book was greatly aided by a Writer's Bursary from the Scottish Arts Council (now Creative Scotland), & a residency at HICA: thanks are gratefully extended.

Thanks also to Cris Cheek, Randolph Healy, Morven Gregor, Tom Leonard, & Peter Manson for their encouragement & suggestions.

fault line

I

about right for these parts
mostly birch
some oak
my living room
where the white hind has
scented me
though I'm glassed in
standard class
on the halted train
through Glen Douglas
she follows my gaze
over her shoulder
to hillside bunkers
trots downwind
in the direction of
the sea's drifting
foam specks
Faslane

while an owl
edits my sleep
an object

II

consider these lilies
what you talk about
when you talk aesthetics
& these sweet coils
woodbine razorwire

my fixed point of the hills
grasping peerless sunlight

III

states of matter
halogen lights
safely do away
with night & day
abolish the moon
barn owl
snatches song
all twenty four hours now
a siren
rock to my hard place
these men talk
to their lapels

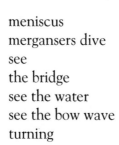

meniscus
mergansers dive
see
the bridge
see the water
see the bow wave
turning

IV

the streets are lined
today I found a penny
yesterday a pound coin
it's on my shopping list
tea wine gold
that everyday hero
Midas
warned me

inadvertently
making the sign
of the cross
on that train
no other
he offers me wine

V

more than one sun
in the sky now
the heron's auguries
no longer to be trusted
she too stands
on the street corner
hand to mouth
hand to ear
I still worry
about the apple trees

dawn
here if
it's rosy fingered
it's brambles
or blood

VI

when his teacher's
lecture
was a flower
between thumb
& forefinger
Kasyapa smiled
I'm collecting
dead bees
from the meadows
above

notice there
a hole
of quietness
knit
by birdsong
by plants' dormancy
by submarines' winches
15 of them
lifting galaxies

VII

the poor boys
of a religious order
are in town
for a drink
& a walk
their fathers
who are not priests
but workers
pushed buttons
with forefingers
detonated

trees' ocean
swell

VIII

what is brought
in the mouths of
lilies of the valley
but spring
it's not that the
bunkers
reamed into the hill
don't wound it
they do
but that geology
is newer
than words in flower
fear piled on fear
how then is anything
possible

true believers
village elders
iconic
mountain ptarmigan

IX

the artist
brought his own stones
to this stony field

in the old east
functional economics
overtakes ancient aesthetics
form follows

X

another heroic struggle
among trees
beith luis fern
sail nin huath
oak & hazel
Sweeney
& the missiles

giddy ripples

XI

evenings spent
shelling beans
early purple orchid
adding interest

when here it must be greeted
when elsewhere celebrated
bruised sky & no sign
of last night's swan
snow on ice the length
of canal east to dawn
white then pink
where else the desert
we will become
that the brain is part
of the body
an intimate struggle
personal dolour

XII

elder
self sown on the
pier's timbers
I saw the Kilcreggan ferry go
run dunlin run
& warships
rounding the point
zulus skiffs & smacks
hulking the shoreline

⇌

look at the breaking day
only the waves not ice
Beinn Bhuidhe white
again silk whistling seven swans
high over frozen waters
magpies clatter mourn
a fallen glacial rook fellow
corvid we burn our
carbon corpses
& the whole sun sinks
in the sea

XIII

why should I leave
Kemp said
why should I travel
I don't even know
my own garden
& still the seedling oaks come
each spring
Colquhouns displacing Gregors
Campbells once more
selling stolen waters
to conquering navies
for their fleets

boreal bright ice
swans wander the strand
seals stravaig the firth
swans paddle the firth
a drift wood forest
salt sparks
the firebox
time
look so
speech is stolen
from truth

XIV

the boat is written
in the leaf

digging for pignuts
don't kill things
what hope the limping
fox in snow
brightness

XV

for the oars:
part the waters
they fold again

fresh water
ice cracks & slams
grips the hull
we make love
name booming gods
crackling stars
her bones

XVI

we took turns making tea
for each other
insurgents
in the woods
spore & stone
& song engines

paired crows
in the bare ash
tree

XVII

I have planted tansy
& angelica
thoughts may be taken
in at the eyes
it can't be said
we were sleeping
we saw the
machines arrive

crows in
one line
bowing
to ice
the exegesis

XVIII

old men greet me
a nod & a smile
in Helensburgh
the chandler
of Rhu is an old friend
of an old friend
we think
they cannot know
my heart

now water under
thin scabs ice crusts
fox & I look
for retreat
neither able
to walk on water
any longer
fox walks
through wood
crows sit on
ice floating rocks
tilt heads in contemplation
sip running water
one of the pleasures
turning on water
turning
on water

XIX

stars
it's true
they came here
by water
once
in Glen Douglas
I saw two white hinds
I thought them sheep
a leaf fell
but we heard
they

⇄

frozen stones
ice slows all waves
even the seventh
who will stop
seagulls'
raucous skrelling
not Neptune
not with his trident
nor any submariner

XX

travel with ghosts
accompany spectres
the sign here reads
report anything suspicious
oak
birch
fern
hazel
be vigilant

⇄

one just
one maybe
the last just
one long
look
ice quelling
water's flows
no other crescent
moon tides

XXI

the ocean's oracle
trident

unspilling to under
this firth bridge
starling clouds
together dispersing night
after night after
seasons' years
again
treatise worlded

XXII

to have loved
to continue loving

to have loved enough
to have loved

to continue love
to have loving

one time
log on riverflow
against tide
modulation
an otter

XXIII

no leaf soars like that
if you skin something
it dies

or is dead

where raw im
permanence stands
the familiar is
not
but ah forget
my fate

XXIV

maybe a small zeus
crying out
until the hills shake
these days
any old developer
or military
cuts his oaks
assassins in the bushes

past the base gate
due south
rattling heavy
along steel rails
engines
at each end
Cerberus
the name plate
no passengers
quotidian driver
barriers
at the crossing

XXV

hunting mushrooms again
in woods by the sea
only black ships slipping
silent through unspeaking water

today now we vote
war lords or
incubi
lines to cross

Hill of Dun
tracked with
who we are
flowering gorse

XXVI

Ruairidh trod
the young lavender down
we forgive children anything
sometimes they become men
in marching boots

on water
turning
caroming on water
one of the pleasures
the bird's
three notes
one two three
one

XXVII

the petals fall
nothing can stop them

the petals fall
there is nothing to stop them

the petals fall
the rose broken

she rises broken hearted
so we change

hammered wedge of geese
cleaving sky through
which leaps as blue split
kindling from my axe

XXVIII

a philosophic stance
to despise landowners
here's one
fencing in rosebay willow herb
& warheads
to keep the berries
from touching ground
we laid them on straw
went at dusk
for the mushrooms

hands wide apart
skein unravelled
what's in mind

XXIX

some of us still live
in the woods
by candlelight
sewing new lines
drinking with hoolets
it will end soon
a knitted glove
no hand

⇌

then
name this one the nucleus
brighter than fission
lighting the woods
bitter sorrel
blood cleanser

XXX

try to write as if for a child try
to write as if
for a politician filching
wells & springs
from the people

what boat
is inside the island
I'm calling coltsfoot
fire

XXXI

it can't be said
of the President
he wouldn't
hurt a fly

a little spark
I eat & name
nettle

XXXII

before the torrents of rain
Bàgh mu Dheas
Bàgh mu Thuath
before the landslides
Rudha nan Sgarbh
Sgeir bhuidhe
leaving aside
the multitudes of frogs
the Hen-house
the Deer Shed
Maggie Baan's Hole
Mecky's Point
now silenced
a people of the sea
the sea

the mast of the riverside
butterbur
named & folded back
& back into the hill
into missiles lodgings

XXXIII

they are not benign
black helicopters
have no ovipositors

& the one for the bird
with two notes
cuckoo flower
oh my slender gun
my blinding sun

XXXIV

efficiently stealing
when I thought I was awake
I left the land music sleeping
throbbing & urgent on
the circular breath of
humans & other creatures
following those narrow paths
that are understood
to lead to the heartland

⇌

water & whisky
& fishmothered garlic
the wood wild blades
chorus themselves

XXXV

a thrush is speaking
tarragon in the garden
it's July 14th
a thrush is speaking all
are born and remain free
and equal in rights
it'd be good to be
smelling buddleia
when the time

⇌

little sister
white bone
earth sap
I name it
hidden carefully
gun cache in green
delayed deferred
broken red straw
berry

XXXVI

two ghettos dreaming
separated by wire
a dream at the front
a dream at the back which
buoys the world
the hinds the hinds
time perhaps to sing

watch the flower rise
as it drinks
sit quietly
it happens
were you on the hill
by the lochan
of concealed soldiers
whisper this one herb
robert

XXXVII

the President jets off
to a far black country
urges the hungry
to consume
& be his friends
the way a landowner
is friends with his fence

one of the banned
names
lus na fola
blood herb
shepherd's purse

XXXVIII

who cleans their ears
while sleeping
to hear dreaming

fliuch some
old words naming
water avens
invocations to rain
also bring wetlands
red wells at the centre
sepal colour is of
beaten bodies

XXXIX

than chanterelles
for supper
& for entertainment
wind
displaying leaves' under
sides
must I ask what slips
past under water
powered & out
into Atlantic depth

law names
plantain
insurrection

XL

how delicate the dove
at the river's edge
quenching a thirst
relentless

I'm just going along
noon naming some of
her names
not stepping on
that one
neòinean
enduring beauty
danger of death
forty thousand volts

XLI

routines
of leaf curl & blossom
ragwort death & panther cap
herons attend
the naval base
raven sits on the fence

⇌

things which know
they know not
ontological
things which know
they know mortality
but sentience
six petalled wood anemone
a split nosed bullet

XLII

concrete
a strange love
to ride the agaric
& what sickens
oil slicked lands
luminous metal water

$$\rightleftharpoons$$

a discourse with piss-a-beds
& pig's snout & cats ear
hawk beard & mouse ear
beàrnan-Bride
Taraxacum I
have no right
to say these things
though no right not to
they nod
a shroud is needed

XLIII

procedures of fatigue

useful rain

XLIV

helicopter helicopter
please come down

between cattle grid &
cattle grid

where mist is farmed
a Depot

behind screened fences
in battle fatigues

they exercise
let the storm come

let theft come
let yarrow come

am I unseen
red flagged

on the hill above
the glen of sorrows

war
games

if you don't come down
I'll shoot you down

not boulders but lambs
not bracken but deer
not sonar but buzzard

XLV

workers
the trade unionist
from central america
talks softly
of repression
heroes as tyrants
a banner
Ulysses must go

air sugared with blossom

XLVI

in his war the General says
there's too few helicopters
the Minister denies this
the ground is littered
with samara
mythological creatures
winged seed

exiled

XLVII

at the head of the glen
just east of the reservoir dam
at a spur of a track
west of power lines
defining ministry land
246935 written
below a triangle
on a scrap of paper
during manoeuvres
Maol Odhar
an unfulfilled prophecy
file & rasp of duck song
click & rattle of magpie
sweet in the ear of the glen

what are the articles (& of war)
falcons on thermals of hot breath
not reasoned but felt
not felt but experienced
not experienced lived
not lived endured

XLVIII

among fleabane
among vetch
among deceivers
at the heart of it

a ring of smoke
a wren's broken eggshell
sea mammal vertebra
fail-chuach
a scented bowl
place enough

XLIX

welcome guests
caterpillar on the dinner kale
snail on a freshly felled tree bole
fires for winter
after next
liberated

in blackness
of a black round moon
there below trees
in head redness throbbing
swans lay their eggs

L

uncountable tormentil
in sward on the hill above
the submarine hangar
once we all
took joy of brambles
stained fingers
lips
now they
have become mighty

the hills scoured
an intrusive morphology
meadows reamed
but have found no orchards

LI

sea mist
lifting a little
black with cancer
a prisoner
goes home to die
the President
declares compassion
to be a mistake

heterophonic
once culture here
psalm 79 sung
unaccompanied
men much given to whisky
crackling in mouths
of farmers the gaelic
chewing thistledown
spitting warheads
none to bury them

LII

driving these roads
I know I'm lost
same fox dead
twice

furze yellow across the hill
what nations in earth
the ploughshare destroys

LIII

what message
from foetid dog's mercury
god of trade
profit and commerce?

then turns grows
& builds climate
near native now
a dish of plums
a big wood dish
of little peppers
another of tomatoes
two oranges
& that lemon-yellow
lemon
furnishing
the press
sun summer
another

LIV

garden news
lambada
thambar
dawn fantasia
& unknown
six blooms
on a board
any cultivar
the lieutenant
is passionate
about fuchsias

he read the left
hand page with the left
eye the right hand page
with the right
here inside
the radio's left ear
Der Rosenkavalier
ah but
ah but right ear's
outside thrush symphony
devoid of moral
likewise summer's
throbbing dragon
flies

LV

meanwhile

he said
smokes after death
she said
smoke takes the eyes
maybe I said
death smokes the eyes

LVI

264 seasons now
I've been watching
it never ceases

begin
to perceive the name
of this plant
how it uses water to
yellow its flowering

then the delicate
traceries in the net
that become
fissionable material

LVII

birches are shedding august
yellow leaves
the President says
there are solutions
geo-engineering
artificial trees

$$\rightleftharpoons$$

talismans & atonements
thumbprints of conscience

LVIII

ever
& pause
bombs spawn here
salmon no longer
make us fearless
any old opiate
or if you wish
whisky

$$\rightleftharpoons$$

thrush there first
crunch underfoot common
snail hard by common
tansy jowl by leaf
with ragwort
the branch that overcomes
is a scythe

LIX

& today
I nailed wood
to wood
then
lit a fire
field maples showed
true colours

they took an eel
a thick forearm
gnarling from the lock
unsewing hook from lip
they bagged it in blue
cornershop polythene
still drinking air
they do this when
I'm not here

grain of the wood
before it's cut
still leafed

indigenous microbiota
flora of the mouth
seven hundred species
a meadow
another attached to skin
no boundary
that side of steel mesh
sanitized annihilation
this side
language seed

LXI

once he was a bishop
once too a boy
daunerin Glen Fruin
a place

not us
not even our view
of us
declining
cockroach
but yellow star
petals fallen on concrete
& tender every year
iadh-lus tenderly
binding
not us
world

LXII

ideology of tridents
fish are dying

go where
songs are sung

$$\rightleftharpoons$$

no epiphanies
reverie
moments aside
scissors paper bone
utter this
gold spangle
Autographa bractea

LXIII

& she who was once a bride
I walk past without checking
my stride

⇌

Lysimachia vulgaris
leaves broad lanceolate
black dotted
sepal toothed
lus-na-sìochaint
peace speaking plant
as if for

LXIV

as if for trees themselves
that conversation
the commons
as if for eels in the sea
as if for gulls
& buzzards in those trees
consciousness
delusional

semantic field
harrowed
large or conspicuous
heads or spikes
in clusters or solitary
star-like
saucer shaped
bell shaped
cup shaped
lusan
common places

LXV

stockpiling
3 bowls on the unlit
autumn stove
green tomatoes
green-red snow white apples
from the tree at the shore
red ripe tomatoes
deterrents

in full bloom
plundered
blàthan
agus plaosgan
seeds left

LXVI

7 herons
in the meadow
horse & rider
cantering
across the bay
by the old fish yair
Gartness fault

he's been by
with the petrol strimmer
by the fence
a foot wide
by 125 paces
ten species
dead or threshed
could name them all
called friends
am I foolish

LXVII

a gannet collapses herself
falls to ocean brim
rheumeyed age plunging
back upwards
officers on deck

splitting wedge
& grafting knife
tongue & pen

LXVIII

how clear shadow is
clearer than lined hand
than veined leaf
than hand bones
held to shade eyes

⇄

stolen expressions
of existence
there's one whose name is lost
Tharsuinn the crosswise hill
& Auchengaich
Chaorach hill of the fank
Maol an Fheidh bleak hill of the deer
the dappled hill
Creag Madaidh little crag of the fox
& the lookout hill of the sheiling
here's the stony hill
the high cracked hill
the red hill & the black hill crowding
litter of the shoreline
Coulport
& Faslane the homestead of sorrows

LXIX

many dogs travel
on the ferry
with passengers
eating breakfast
watching clouds
mushroom

sudden oak death
& they're on edge
round the corner
deep horizon
never to apprehend
the abundant numinous
now

LXX

kyrie kyrie
in greenblue confusion
a kingfisher
singing a pitched song
sounding like anger
to those out of tune
compressed signals
the frequency of
windscream in halyards

to act is
to dream
what is said
by the invisible

LXXI

the Minister calls
for a lesser capacity
to kill 38 million people
not the full 51 million
the President smiles

paper not stone
skin not paper
brain and skin
who'ld stop the
leaves swarming
he asked

LXXII

a lute
hanging in a wind
bent blackthorn
on autumn
fugitive hills
gods & heroes
like any other refugees
the President smiles again
solvet saeculum in favilla

gu'n airigh
at the high
summer pastures
wood sorrel
for children
transhumance
cup & ring marks
bullet pocks

LXXIII

gulls follow the plough
that guns be used
only for the firing of seeds
willowherb down
as if for
borrowed time
the day's work
6 coach screws
sent home into
roof trusses
free//for less
than a clock's single tock
ashes postponed

going backwards
dances of hills
movements
& the verb
of the cold hill
the bald hill

this lyre
this lute bothers me
not even sweet
as a swan hooting
through her nostrils
feet slapping water in
the effort to fly
to sing to rise

⇌

suddenly
since it's all not there
there's nothing
no harebell
no hill
as sudden
there's hill
there's summer
furze
no thing
unadorned unborn
mind
but caring what happens
as if for love
practising
as if for compassion
don't be scared
as if for a single
raindrop
out in the firth

LXXV

blue to green
to blue
the artist says

beyond steel
beyond altar
elegance & pain
rockforms
walking

LXXVI

some unqualified days
late roses
October sun
pass with no thought
of coffined boys
back from war

grist to the mill
mill gone
sea pink sea thistle
an entropic descant
flux

LXXVII

this morning's transecting flights
two silkwinged swans
above a platefat mallard
below a seaplane

ending sentience
country sports
for pleasure
not the oldest
way here

LXXVIII

it's 6am October
an invention
moon's high
not shot down
breath forming inside
my body

every farmer a connoisseur
of rusty machinery
ploughshares
chased by rainbows
sifting foliage

LXXIX

the Players
begin wakening
stretch to
immediate caffetieres
toast & mobiles
text mntns
meaning not mountains
not Beinn Chaorach
gathering frost
but munitions

the hand that targets
the army
will be cut off
the Leader says
the tree
a spruce
points the first limb
across the fence

LXXX

all the little cancers sing
in the sheepfold
More Power is dead
in the sheiling
Bikini Frank
is dead
move over lyric

⇌

another Sunday
we sit
baking the word
of god
on the steel hull
gulls yell
a' ghràidh

LXXXI

lately made of flesh & blood
in Operation Herrick
the Major tells us
how remarkably
this irrigation system
so closely resembles
that of the valley
of the river H
& straw & manure
& here's a number of the
A diaspora too

what's the dance we are left with
after hours whisky
what's the song bequeathed
a red rose
then he says
salmon in a tin
venison on butcher slab
what's the ground we're left with
bracken & ragwort
nightshade

LXXXII

officers cleansing
anarchic habitats
their real enemy
Flora being goddess

shorten the road for me
he was ever a child
as if for those who went before
& then the boys jump
feet first
into the stars of
blackened sky

LXXXIII

aside from us
who will celebrate
shoreline's windfall
apples

it's only the foxes
in waterside herbs
& herself
sits out
looking for
cosmic debris
perseids

LXXXIV

the birds decline to read

& he's thinking
as if for
as if

LXXXV

do you remember
that sun rising
that threnody
how urgently
they broke the news
mute swan
shrieking heron
rasping crow
curlew & redshank
keening running
at the ragged selvedge
where sand
is no longer mountain
not yet sea

going out
these days
just to buy wine

LXXXVI

the sycamore
cuts off
from her leaves
in scarlet they are
vibrant
soon to fall
the Peer declares
forgiveness a mistake
the Priest agrees
it's trite

bubbles from the ears
drownded
as we used to say
daily navigators
never mind Brendan
all but gone
Gare Loch Loch Long
we build land rivers
from the cemetery
to the snow gate
above the glen
fast to the A82
for messengers of war
fast south
reinforcements
fast north

LXXXVII

here for the chirr & rattle
of a starling
slow fall of her song
leaf to note leaf
saved lives
shortened the war
dropping those bombs
numbers
the Engineer says
talks of swans & carp
while stripping wires

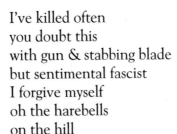

I've killed often
you doubt this
with gun & stabbing blade
but sentimental fascist
I forgive myself
oh the harebells
on the hill

LXXXVIII

that way sea smells
take nothing more

jumping the gun
has no equivalent
in the old language
old fellers then
called it
pre-emptive strike
or maybe
cracking
broom seed pods

LXXXIX

after Schoenberg's Gurrelieder
fields shorn after harvest
Drumfad cattle & crows fat
Tam-na-voulin's wind
Duirland's cock pheasant
Ballevoulin snuff coloured tups & steers
fanks of Auchengaich
wheels

⇌

expect revolutionary
proletarian advice
from these swans
a monarch claims them
as property

XC

stirring soup
4 railway carriages slip by

standards lowered

we have the right
to start a war
it's our right
to self-defense
the MP says
how sleek the crows are
this year

XCI

honeybees at the ivy balls
sweetness giving messages
back at the hive dancing
numbers
litter of pollen

to be unseen on waters
invisible against ripe
wheat fields
why kingfishers are blue
goldfinches gold
at borders if I had a gun
would I tell you
the correct answer
do not joke
about bombs while
in an airport
it is an offence

XCII

there's only one river
& we & all always in it
chaffinch crowd
at fallen rowan berries
still they refuse to read
we have different texts
sometimes they speak of me
of men with arms
warning to their kind
a psalter lies
open at this page
there is only one river
fieldfares speak//sing
of the same rowan
when all's clear
of the buzzard
when she's gone

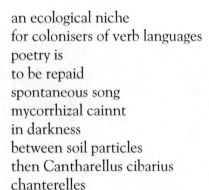

an ecological niche
for colonisers of verb languages
poetry is
to be repaid
spontaneous song
mycorrhizal cainnt
in darkness
between soil particles
then Cantharellus cibarius
chanterelles

XCIII

light does not fall
night does not fall
night rises
as dawn rises
twilight becomes
arriving

⇌

why go to the foreshore
apples fall there
how does the moon turn us round
she dwells in us
how does Aquila fix the sky
with burnished copper
how does Fulica stitch flat water
with the yarn of our mothers
what is to be done with the Cygnus dust of a dead star
pass by

XCIV

at once buzzard & thrush
a peace machine
only our names being born

what I would ask
is this
is that
why does the dipper dwell in speech

XCV

birch a palimpsest
on this window
they thing themselves
in silence
not speech

this side that side
fence more
holes than wire
welcome mice
gnaw the store of apples
Beauty of Moray
Galloway Pippin
Scotch Bridget
& the others

XCVI

only the physical act
of sitting
through that window
hare's gorging
on fallen rowan berries
who asks the twig
about attrition
rather address the tree
in another view
to the east
armed thieves
still at the water
taking 6 times
the others' pint

what is the form
of frost rising into all
these trees
what is the shape of a war
of a warhead
of a fountainhead of rising frost
what is

XCVII

incandescence
as they wish
we don't want
what they wish
nevertheless
language is language
spoken
a response
a condemnation
more than despair
to be deleted
the hare tells us
what the lurcher knows

what directs
the sun
what directs your heart
what directs
this fusion
of both
of all

XCVIII

once there were 5 hares loupin
preoccupation with numbers
a retreat from enormity
an occupation
how to meet force

who sees

XCIX

then naming what
being the opposite of
war let's call it
not a wish to oppose
but to circumvent perhaps
to find roots (we know it's fear)
is it as he said
not peace
maybe then an obliquity the dog
sitting on the back
of the shepherd's vehicle
to grasp failure
& wring a damp success
not enough

⇄

what arises
empty of what
sometimes a woman
sometimes a man

C

yet again it's morning
the sun comes up over that hill
the wild cock pheasant
who frequents this yard is busy
at grains the hens have overlooked
with their glassy stare
as children let's begin
eyes ears nose & throat
lips tongue hands & feet
dance my little laddy
the shepherd takes a stick my child
the farmer takes a plough
the soldier takes a gun my dear
& then he shoots your daddy

consciousness delayed
deferred
from under deep snow
shining
Bellis perennis
said before
to be said again
beyond
the always beautiful
beyond together
beyond while still here
no eye ear nose tongue body or mind
no form sound smell taste touch
no extinction

so I've heard